This story is dedicated to my Father, Robert Truman Murphy (1920-2017), who encouraged me to write it. He set the bar high as he wrote his memoirs in his late 80's and early 90's that was put into book form by my younger brother Steve, and was available for sale on Amazon. He thought that maybe someone, such as my grandchildren, would be interested in my story. Dad was a World War II Naval combat veteran, a husband to my Mom, Margaret Anne Horr Murphy for 68 years, and father to 5 children. He was a successful businessman, rising to manage the large tire manufacturing plant that employed his father as a tire builder, and later owned his own management consulting business.

That Murphy Boy

Early Years

I guess I was always very active or a little wild growing up. I wonder if that came from the story of my beginning that was told to me as I got older. Dad and Mom decided they would get married at the first opportunity, war or no war. Dad's ship, the USS Aulick, was going to return to the states in late 1943, so Dad got word to Mom. Her Mother, Maud Anderson Horr, was able to plan a wedding on a short notice. After the wedding, Mom and Dad went back to the west coast for a short honeymoon while waiting for his ship to head out to sea again. Word came, and Dad shipped out at Christmas, 1943. Mom then took the train back to Ohio by herself. Some time after the ship got to sea, it hit a huge storm. It was so bad that Dad told about carrying a large can around to get sick in as he and other sailors carried on their duty while the ship plunged in and out of the huge waves. After all, being sea sick was no excuse for missing a watch in the Navy. The severe storm damaged the ship so much it had to limp back to port. Again, he got word to Mom that he was coming back. She arrived sometime in February, 1944. I was born in late November, 1944, so you can do the math. So the timing of my birth was due to a large storm in the Pacific Ocean.

The name of this story came from the person who later became my mother-in-law. Once I was chasing a kid with a bull whip who had been bothering my younger brothers. I had made the whip at Scout Camp by braiding leather pieces together and had gotten pretty good at making the whip crack over my head by swinging it around, then quickly reversing direction. Done right, the whip would make quite a sound. I was not trying to strike the kid, but to scare him off and run him back up the hill to his own neighborhood. He lived near what was my future wife's family, hence years later I heard about "that Murphy boy" name. Somehow Sally's Mom found out about the chase and used that name. I would have been in junior high school at that time, since we only lived in that house which was just down a hill from the Curchin's for a little over two years.

I was either not afraid to try new, daring things, or a little crazy – you will have to decided that. I always liked to climb trees – the higher the better, although only one of my 4 broken arms came from only a 3 foot fall when I caught my foot in a fork in a tree as I was almost to the ground. It got so I knew the special pain from a broken bone, and would go home to tell Mom that I broke an arm. I don't remember how she dealt with the other children at home while she took me to the doctor. The other arms got broken by jumping off a swing, falling off a board crossing a ditch at a new house under construction next door to us, and later as an adult when Sally and I were biking on the Outer Banks of North Carolina. She went off the edge of the pavement and fell. I was too close to her, and ran into her and also fell. I chipped my elbow – she was fine. I also broke my left leg when I was wrestling with some neighbor kids in my late twenties. They were holding onto my leg while another pushed me sideways to the ground. Something snapped, which was my left fibula. Fortunately, the doctor put a walking cast on the leg which enabled me to continue working in my print shop. More about the print shop later.

Other injuries involved a cut on my chin from flying over my handlebars after going full-tilt down a hill and hitting a big bump which caused the bike to stop. Of course, I didn't stop, and hit the pavement with my chin. I still remember going into a grocery store with blood streaming down my front and asking for a towel. The scar is still there from the healed cut and stitches. I was probably 8 at the time.

Another much more serious injury came during the summer between my 4th and 5th grades, which would have made me 10. I was staying over night at my cousin Tim's house out in the country. We were going to build a little town complete with paved roads out in their orchard. We found some old shingles and thought that we could melt the tar off the shingles and use that to pave the roads. We put the shingles in a can and poured some gas in and lit it. It was burning, but started to go out, so I told Tim I'd pour some more gas on it. The trouble is, I spilled some gas on my right leg and it immediately caught fire. I had been trained in Scouts to drop and roll if you caught fire – the trouble is I was rolling so fast that my cousin couldn't catch me to jump on and smother the fire. Some weeks later I went to his house and still could see the charred path through their orchard where I was rolling. Either Tim finally got me, or the fire burned out. The jeans I had on were not burned, but when we looked under them at the rear of my right calf, it didn't look good. My aunt took me to my house, where my Dad took me to the hospital. There was hardly any pain, and I remember on the way home saying that it didn't look too bad. I can only wonder what my parents thought. I remember Dad saying later that when the doctor told him he was going to remove some of the burned skin, that he was afraid it would be very painful – but it wasn't. I was in the hospital several weeks that time, then twice more during the school year for a week or so for skin grafts. To add insult to injury, it was decided that along with the second skin graft I would be circumcised. I had lots of injections, mostly with antibiotics, which we called "shots." I tell nurses these days when I need to get a shot that they don't hurt a bit, because I got lots of them when I was a kid, and not with new, small needles as they use today. When I was allowed out of bed, I got very proficient in racing around in a wheelchair. The burns were from first to third degree, and I still have the scars from it. I was very self-conscious about the scars for years. I still remember going home for the first time that my heel wouldn't come down so I would run around on my right toe. As time went on though, the achilles tendon stretched back out and I had no more issues with it.

We lived right on the edge of farm land, so during the summers we would roam the fields and woods, catching frogs and butterflies. We would put the bugs in a jar with some carbon tetrachloride on a cotton ball to kill them quickly. Of course much later we learned how dangerous that chemical was. I seemed to be too fascinated with fire. Once when I was very young, I took some matches to a field across the road, and for some reason, lit some and placed them in a pile of dried grass. Needless to say, the fire began to spread, and as my Dad and other men ran with shovels and rakes to fight the fire, he stopped long enough to give me a spanking as I ran home. In the fall when the corn in the fields were dry, we would pick some ears and get the kernels off. Then when we went trick-or-treating we would throw the dry corn up on a porch, which made a nice racket for the residents. If nobody was home, we would soap the windows. Somehow we discovered that paraffin wax would be better to put on the windows because it would not wash off with water. My Mom would can vegetables and fruit and would seal the jars with paraffin, so we always had a supply of it. My buddies and I would always talk about more tricks we could pull on Halloween, but never went through with them.

We would get to sleep out in the back yard some nights during the summer. Several buddies and I would all do it on the same night in our own yards , then sneak out in the middle of the night and roam around the neighborhood. I don't remember doing anything bad except pulling some carrots from a man's garden and eating them after we washed them off. It was just exciting to be out sneaking around.

Another childhood escapade involved cutting down some neighbor's trees. Evidently I was old enough to have an axe, but not old enough to realize that the wooded lot might be owned by someone. A couple of buddies and I thought we'd cut down some trees and make a kind of fort. We had several small ones cut down when we were stopped by the owner, who later told our parents. I don't remember what they had to do to make it right for the owner. I proved the old adage true: you give a boy an axe and he'll chop something. Another old adage was also true: you give a boy a BB gun and he'll shoot something. A couple of us would go out in a field and have a war with each other - shooting at each other. Trouble was, my one buddy had a pump gun which has much more power than my old Red Ryder, so it would sting badly if he hit me. I guess we were all lucky that we never put someone's eye out. Later, in grade school, for some unknown reason another buddy and I decided we'd shoot at an old man who lived near the buddy who was a real grouch. I don't remember who made the shot that hit the man in the hand, drawing blood. He called the cops who came and took a report, but I don't remember what the outcome of that was. I don't think my parents ever knew since it was at the other guy's house.

As children, we kids each had one food that we didn't like and weren't required to eat. All other food on our plate we had to eat, no matter how long it took. Dad would quote something that was in the dining room on the ship: "Take all you want, but eat all you take." Trouble is, if I didn't take anything - it was served to me. I still remember choking down green beans one at a time. My food to skip was liver. I couldn't stand the smell or texture of it. It was thought by some then and still today as good for you, but organ meats never appealed to me. Dad mixed up some sauce of mustard and ketchup and tried to get me to try that. I did, but it didn't help. I only learned many years later that he didn't like liver either so the sauce was for him more than us.

My family had a cottage at Lakeside, Ohio where we would spend some weekends, and an occasional week during the summer. At times much of the extended family was there. Once when I was about 4, I was outside one evening after dark playing with my two older cousins, Tom & Tim. Some other young boy was bothering us, so we climbed up onto a roof of a small hut used as storage for the tennis court equipment. The kid was trying to climb up after us, so my cousins said, "Mike, pee on him." I was too young to know better, so I did. The kid ran home crying, and later we went back to our cottage. It wasn't long before there was an angry knock at the door. When the door was answered, it was the boy's mother who told my parents what I had done. I got a spanking and was sent to bed. Shortly after, as I lay in bed still crying, my Grandpa Murphy came up and into my room. He told me he knew it wasn't all my fault, and gave me a dime. I remember Grandpa as a jovial man who always had a smile. He would go hunting with an uncle on Thanksgiving morning so there would always be rabbit on the table along with turkey. Even as a kid that didn't appeal to me. A story is told about me being with him once in late winter when I was very young. He thought I said that my nose was all gone. After questioning me several times, realized that I was saying that the snow was all gone - just wasn't pronouncing the "s". Grandpa died of cancer when I was in the third grade. It was the first time I saw my Dad cry.

I remember my Grandfather Horr, my Mom's Dad, as a gentle man who could whistle and sound like a train. Back then many trains were still steam locomotives, and when we would visit in Portsmouth, my Mom's home town, we would hear the trains at night. Grandfather was in World War I as a member of the Red Cross. He also owned a building supply business in Portsmouth, where I was born when my Dad was at sea during the war. One year when I was very young I remember him visiting us in Mansfield. Unfortunately, he died of a heart attack when I was in the first grade, so I don't have more memories of him. My brother Scott had, as his middle name, Grandpa Murphy's first name of Willard. My brother Steve had Grandfather Horr's first name of Arthur as his middle name. Of course my middle name is from my Dad.

I got proficient at mumbly-peg, where you would throw a knife in various ways so the blade would stick in the ground. You would start off on each elbow, knee, etc. I found that my Scout knife with the leather punch out had the best balance and was less likely to cut you if you slipped. Another knife game was to stand facing another guy with your feet apart and throw the knife as close to his feet as you could, without of course hitting him. I don't remember anyone ever getting hurt with that game.

Of course bike riding was a big thing, and we road all over

the country side. Once several of us, including my younger brother Scott, were riding down a gravel lane on a farm, when Scott hit a rock and fell. He said his knee hurt, but I told him to get back on his bike and ride home. Later, his knee swelled badly so Dad took him to the hospital were blood was drawn off his knee and a full cast was put on his leg. I felt badly about that.

I loved anything with wheels and a motor. I recall when my Dad got our first power mower. I couldn't wait to get home from school to mow the lawn. I was supposed to stay after school to attend a Cub Scout pack meeting, but I told them I had to go home to mow the grass. When I showed up at home, I had to tell my Mom what happened. She made me wait till Dad got home to tell him I lied.

Another time my Dad had the idea of a way for me to make some money to save for college. I would go to houses and ask them if they had any old tires in their garage, and if so, I'd pay them $5 each for them. Then I would take them to my Uncle's tire recapping business and he would give me $10 each,. I had save up $40 or so that was kept on my dresser. One day my Dad noticed that money was not there. When he asked me what happened to it, I had to admit that some of us had found an old motorcycle that we all chipped in to buy. It was a hunk of junk that barely ran, and of course we were all too old to legally drive one, but we bought it and worked on it. I had to give up my part of the ownership but the money was gone.

My Dad was promoted to become the plant manager of a Mansfield Tire affiliate, Pacific Tire in Oakland, California. Before we were going to move to California, my Dad went to begin the new position early while Mom got things wrapped up at home. School started in California, but since we were moving soon, I didn't start the 9th grade in Mansfield. For some reason I was left to be able to run around during the day for a week or so. Another kid who was cutting school and I knew where 2 mopeds were kept during the day while the owners were in school. It was easy to get the lock off the front fork then start them up. We had a great time riding them all round town. We weren't stealing, just borrowing them because we'd take them back each afternoon. Of course, someone told on me and the kid was not too happy. I ended up in juvenile court with my Mom and distinctly remember the judge chewing me out for making my young mother cry. I don't remember any police being involved or any punishment as we were moving away soon. I always wondered why such a big deal was made out of this since there was no actual harm or damage done. Years later when I was reading some memoirs my Dad wrote, I saw that when they were going to build a new house in Mansfield, a contractor they were talking do was not given the job because they thought he was too expensive. I read that he was the father of the kid who's moped I borrowed. Maybe there was some sour grapes involved and some pay back.

One thing that I enjoyed for years was playing music on my tenor saxophone. I first got a used alto sax from an uncle while I was in grade school and took some private lessons. In junior high I played in the concert band as well as the marching band. I got good enough to become the first chair. At some time in junior high my Dad bought me a brand new sax which I enjoyed and still have, although I haven't played it in years. Near the end of the 8th grade I was approached by the band director to become the drum major for the next year. I was told it was because I fit the uniform. I thought it might be neat to lead the band around the field wearing the uniform and big hat. Of course I would have to learn to twirl, throw and catch a baton to do that. I spent quite some time that summer with some of the majorettes who gave me lessons. That was not to be as Dad got transferred. I played the sax for years after, in the marching band at the high school in California, then in the school dance band. We played lots of the big band music that was popular in the 40's such as "In The Mood." I played some at Ohio State to accompany a couple of guys in the fraternity who were trying to get chosen as a May King or something like that. They had to go around and sing at sorority houses and women's dorms. I even played some year later with some guys from the parish I served in Richmond as a 50's and 60's oldies band. That band played at our children's weddings.

A highlight of my life, which I didn't realize at the time, was when Sally's Dad took a job in Mansfield and moved his family to my home town. As alluded to earlier, they moved less than 100 yards from where we lived in the new house, but it was up a hill past some other houses, so I didn't notice the new people moving in. I began to notice this interesting new girl who was running around with some of the kids I ran around with. Since there were several elementary schools feeding students into the junior high school, there were lots of kids I didn't know, so I never realized at the time that she had moved from out of state.

I mentioned Scouts. One of the the things I enjoyed most growing up was being in Boy Scouts. Going to camp in the summer was a real treat, and I would work on merit badges. In fact, I got enough that I got my Eagle rank at age 14 just before we moved to California. One night at camp, we were in our tent talking late. There must have been some cussing going on. Suddenly a counselor burst in the tent and took us all to clean out the grease pit as a punishment for our cussing. The pit was where all the cooking grease went, and had a foul smell – which was a fitting punishment for what we were doing. Somehow we missed the "morally straight" section of the Scout oath.

One summer I spent a week at Lakeside with my Grandma Murphy - just the two of us. Grandma was always fun to be with, and a very generous person. She always had a stick of gum to give you. I remember we went on a speed boat ride one evening while there. Who would think that a junior-high aged boy would want to spend a week with his grandmother? Some years after she died, my Dad showed me her check book register. The last entries were Christmas checks made out to me and her other grandchildren. The balance that was left was less than $5. That epitomizes Grandma.

As mentioned previously, before I began the ninth grade, my Dad got transferred to be the plant manager at the Oakland, California tire plant, so my family moved to Danville, somewhat east of Oakland. I went from going to be the top dog – a ninth grader in a 7-9 grade junior high school, to a lowly 9th grader in a 9-12 grade high school. That might have contributed to my wanting to fit in with the kids I ran around with. We got to see some great places during the 2 ½ years there, but I got into some stuff that could have had very serious negative consequences on my life. One thing that caused friction between my Dad and me was the style out there for guys to let their hair grow longer - not down to the shoulders as became popular in the 70's, but long on the sides and swept back in a "duck tail" kind of like was seen on the Fonz in the popular TV show "Happy Days." For a time I had what was called a "flat top with fenders" which was a flat top on top but the sides long and swept back. Then for a time it was long on top also, but still the swept back sides. I know my Dad didn't like it as I still remember him showing me a cover of Sports Illustrated one time that had a photo of Dick Butkus on it, with his short butch hair cut. Dad's hair wasn't cut like that, but he thought mine should go back to that style as it once was. But, I wanted to fit in, and getting a bad case of acne made me even more self conscious.

I stayed in Scouts after we first moved to California, being appointed as the Junior Assistant Scout Master of the troop there. A neat experience we had was a weekend camping trip to Angel Island, in the middle of San Francisco Bay. You could hear the fog horns moaning all night, which was a new experience for me. I also caught a number of star fish and brought them home to dry out. I didn't stay in Scouts for long after. One reason was that the Scout Master seemed to make me his personal cook, which I didn't like. Also, being in Scouts was just not cool with the guys I ran around with.

California was of course totally different in climate and geography than I was used to in Ohio. It got dry in the summer, then would rain a lot in the winter. The heat was dryer, so I don't remember it as uncomfortable. In winter it would get into the 50's. Kids were wearing winter coats like it was really cold. We lived in the San Ramon valley which was east of Oakland. Out our front window we saw the Los Trampas hills, and in the back, Mt. Diablo. At least once each winter clouds would cover Mt. Diablo, and when they would clear, snow would cover the peak. They would actually close schools so the kids could go up on the mountain and play in the snow. I never did that as I had plenty of experience with snow in Mansfield.

Another time I had a Sparrow Hawk. I don't know how I came to have it, but I built a cage in the back yard and had it trained to fly around then come back and land on my arm when I whistled for it. I would threaten my brother Scott, saying I would teach the hawk to attack the pigeons he was raising. I doubt though that the sparrow hawk could or would attack a bird that size. I used raw liver for a training aid, which further deepened my dislike for eating liver. Of course hawks are not meant to be kept in captivity, and the bird started banging his head against his cage, wearing off some feathers. We went on a trip for a couple of weeks, so I had some buddy take care of it for me. Somehow, he left the cage open and the bird escaped. I always wonder if he did that on purpose. I had one other experience with a hawk - this time a Red Tail. A buddy of mine wanted to take a young one from a nest, so we climbed high in a tree, and I kept shooing the mother away so he could grab the young bird. Naturally the mother didn't like us taking one of her babies, but she never physically attacked us. It was a little scary though as she would scream and dive right at you. It is surprising how big a Red Tail Hawk actually is when it is sitting on your arm.

In our first house, my Dad had an assortment of cigars in the garage, so occasionally I would take one out and go smoke it. One kind had a chocolate tasting inner wrapper. I don't remember getting sick from doing that. Since smoking was not such a health issue back then, many kids, including me, would start smoking too young when we could get away with it. You could buy them easily, or sneak them from your parents. Once when we lived in California, for some reason I climbed up a tree onto the roof of our one-story house and started smoking a cigarette. Somehow, I dropped it and watched while it rolled down the roof onto the patio below. Unfortunately, my parents were sill sitting at the dining table finishing Sunday dinner when this lit cigarette fell onto the patio and rolled away right in front of them. It was hard to explain that away, so I had no choice but to admit what I was doing when Dad called to me.

Another dumb thing that I did while living in California was to take the family car out for a joy ride with my buddies a couple of times when my parents went out. I would put my younger brother Scott in charge, then go and pick the guys up and roar around town. The trouble was, I was only 15 and didn't have a license. The last time I did that, we were out in the country and we wanted to make the tires squeal when we took off from a stop. So I revved up the engine in park, then threw the transmission down into drive. Unfortunately, there was a loud clunk and the car began making a terrible noise. I limped home after dropping off the guys and put the car in the garage. All the next day I worried about what was going to happen to me. When I went home, Mom said the car was making a strange noise so she took it to a garage where she was told the rear end had some teeth broken out. I never admitted it, and perhaps they could never imagine what I did. Many years later my brother told on me.

The guys I ran around with in California were not the best influence, and as I said before, I wanted to fit in at the new school too much. During my sophomore year in high school, one guy discovered that his dad had a case of Jack Daniels whiskey in the closet which was given to him by a client. He would take a bottle out and we would go to to a lumber yard on Friday night and pass it around and chase it with soda. Even though it was supposed to be good whiskey, we'd all gag as we drank it. Then we would go to the football game. Real fun!

One time during my sophomore year some of my buddies

and I thought it would be neat to put a big "Class of '62" sign up some place on the high school campus. We got a 4 x 8 sheet of plywood and painted that on it. Since I was not afraid of heights, I tied the sign on my back, and climbed up one of the high light poles that illuminated the football field. The sign could be seen all over the high school grounds. Needless to say, the upper class people didn't like it, but my buddies kept quiet about who did it. The sign stayed up for over a week before the school got it taken down.

We would occasionally hitch hike over to Oakland to buy some maple flavored cigarettes, or to neighboring Walnut Creek. One day for some reason I went by myself to Walnut Creek and was walking through a department store when I saw a key ring with a large "M" on it. I looked around and saw nobody watching me, so I picked it up and put it in my pocket. As I started walking away, a strong hand grabbed my arm. I looked around to see a lady store security person. She took me upstairs and called the police. An officer came and took me to the police station, were I sat in a room until my Dad came to pick me up. There were no charges, but I sure learned my lesson. I remember listening to Mom & Dad talking about it after dinner, and Dad saying that he wondered what they did wrong for me to do something like that. I thought to myself that it wasn't them - they were great parents - it was just me being a stupid teenage kid. Once again I proved that just knowing the right thing to do didn't mean a person would do it. I certainly was raised to know right from wrong, but I often didn't do what was right.

The same guy who got the Jack Daniels had gotten an old Model T and Model A Ford from his grandfather. His dad had a garage built in the back yard in which we spent hours working on those cars. We got the Model T running and rode in it in the "Hay Days" parade through town dressed like hillbillys. I've got some of our old home movies that show that parade. We put a V-8 engine in the Model A and racing slicks on the rear end, and had a ball driving around in it, especially riding in the rumble seat.

Ohio & Sally

Each summer we would take a trip back to Ohio to visit relatives. The train ride through the mountains was especially memorable, as were trips to Disney Land and Yosemite. One summer on the trip back east I want to a former girl friend's house and Sally was there. Again, she intrigued me. Then in the fall of 1960 Dad asked if we would mind moving back to Mansfield as he was offered the plant manager job in the main plant. I've told him before that I was relieved – I didn't think I'd end up well if we stayed in California. So back we went.

A couple other examples of my fascination with wheels and motors came when I was finally old enough to drive legally. I talked my parents, when they were going to buy a new Ford Station wagon, to get one with a stick shift. I loved driving that. A buddy and I would unhook the muffler from the exhaust pipe and drive around with all the racket that an engine makes with no muffler, like we had a hot rod. We also wanted to make the car faster, so got larger jets for the carburetor and installed them. It was just a 2 barrel, so didn't do much except make the car use more gas. Dad had a company car which was an Oldsmobile super 88. You wouldn't think that was a car a teenager would like, but it was real fast. I would take off the air cleaner, and the 4 barrel would make the neatest noise when I tromped on the gas.

In some ways going back to my home town was like starting over. I had missed 2 ½ years of the experience that my old buddies had gone through. Sally was dating the quarter back of the football team. However, in chemistry lab, her seat was right next to mine. I began dating another girl for awhile, but she dumped me for the guy Sally had dated. Then one afternoon right before our senior year, some of us were at a picnic at a local lake. Sally was there and the two of us ended up swimming together. My interest in her grew. Shortly after I asked her out to a movie, but I since I was the oldest of 3 boys, I was always awkward around girls. I didn't have sense enough to ask her out again. Time went on and she dated another guy for a time. Then in the late fall of 1961, for some reason I got up my nerve and asked her out, even though she was still dating the other guy. For some reason, she said yes. We've been together since then. Now as you can see, I've done some dumb stuff – some dangerous stuff, and much more than I've told about here, but that was the best thing I've every done.

One thing we did our first weeks and months together was to go ice skating on a local small lake in a park in Mansfield. Sally was a much better skater than I, but I could go forward pretty well and stop when needed. We would be on the lake many evenings skating and when a freight train went by we would fantasize about hopping the train and seeing the country. In some ways that is what we are doing now as we travel in our RV. More about that later.

Sally went off to a junior college 600 miles away in upstate New York, and I went to Ohio State. I had written a paper in high school English class about the famous architect, Frank Lloyd Wright, and I thought I wanted to be an architect. In my pre-admission testing for OSU I was told I needed to go to Columbus during the summer and take remedial math. Now I had gotten A's in Trigonometry and Solid Geometry my senior year so that puzzled me. Also, Sally and I were soon to be separated by 600 miles, so I was not going to be gone our last summer together, so I changed my major to business.

My grades were not good, so after 2 years I was through with OSU. Sally's 2 year course was done, so we were married. I don't remember a fancy proposal like you see on TV. We had picked out rings, and on her birthday in 1964 I gave her a ring. Our wedding was on Thanksgiving weekend and was very nice and much of the extended family was there. I was a nervous wreck as my future mother-in-law enjoyed teasing me about what was planned for the service. I was told later that a younger cousin got into the champagne at the reception, and got sick. Dad was my best man and took pains to hide my car so there would not be any messing with it. We took our honeymoon in Niagara Falls in late November. My Dad asked me if I had enough money for the trip. I had $50 so he gave me his Standard Oil Credit Card for gas. I don't know how we made the trip on that amount of money.

I was only given two days off for the wedding plus the weekend, as I had just gotten my first real job as a shipping clerk with the local General Motors plant. I had also worked summer jobs as a laborer in a brick yard and a steel mill. The job entailed shift work. I hated 2nd and especially 3rd shift. I was back on day shift when one day my boss came to me and said I had to go back to 3rd shift as they had hired a new person and had to train them on day shift. That made me so mad that I gave my 2 week notice. I went home and told Sally I had quit. I'm surprised she didn't leave me, as she had just had Sarah, our first child. I wasn't exactly providing a secure living for my new family.

Printer

At a dinner with my parents soon after, I told them I had quit my job. Dad had recently begun a management consulting and training business and to help with all the printing that was needed in teaching courses, had bought a printing press. Then an old friend of his and he decided to make more use of the press and opened a quick printing business. They had talked about franchising that type of business, since most printing companies were not equipped for small, fast jobs at that time. Dad talked about me coming to work with them to learn the business, and after a couple of years, to open a franchise shop in another town. In 3 months I thought I knew enough, and after looking for a place to rent in Sandusky and Columbus, chose Columbus. A relative of an old friend had an insurance business in Columbus, and told me he would give me his printing business if I moved there. Dad cosigned a $3000 loan so I could buy some equipment and have some working capital. For October and November of 1966 I drove to Columbus 3 days a week to solicit business, then brought it back to Mansfield to produce it. I found a store front to rent in late November so drove to Columbus every day in December to run the business. My Dad and brothers had helped me move the equipment down there. Then we moved to our home on New Year's Eve 1966 with the help of my two brothers. I was one of 150 printers in Columbus and I was not even in the yellow pages for almost a year. I had to get business by making cold calls and through direct mail. The business slowly grew. We moved 3 times to rental houses, and finally bought our first home in 1970. I had to get a cash advance on a credit card to make the down payment. During those years, our other two children, Rebecca and Michael, Jr. were born.

Although I was taught the basics of offset printing by a man who worked for Dad, I had to teach myself much of the business. For example, without a darkroom, if I needed a metal plate for a longer run, I had to take it to a company who specialized in that type of work. I wanted to be more independent, so modified my camera to use film, and built a dark room to I could handle the film in the low light conditions necessary for it. I learned how to make films of photos and how to make my own metal plates. This saved money and was faster. Anytime I got a new piece of equipment I had to learn how to use it. I bought a larger offset press so I could run larger jobs. One advantage was that you could get 4 regular sheets on one large 17 x 22 piece of paper, then cut them apart, saving time on larger runs. You could also print booklets that way. I remember holding the instruction manual in one hand while I ran the press.

I also did some things that probably should have been left to professionals. For example, when I built the darkroom, I needed to move the gas space heater. That involved iron pipe that had to be re-routed to the new location. It actually wasn't too hard to do once I bought a pipe wrench and pipe dope. I tested for leaks by holding a match to the joint rather than using soapy water like a pro would have done. No flame, no leak. Another time I had to run some new electric current to a power paper cutter that I had bought. I had 220 volt, 3 phase current run into the shop to power the larger press I had purchased, but I had to run the same current to the cutter which sat in the front of the shop. Running the conduit was not difficult but was time consuming. Hooking up the current from the box so it would run to the cutter was something I should have left to an electrician, but I was always too willing to try something new as well as save a few bucks. For years afterward, I had the screw driver that had a weld mark on it where I accidently touched the metal to the side of the box as I was tightening one of the wires. The large spark and noise when it touched made me jump and I was thankful that my fingers were not touching the driver, or I probably would not be writing this.

The broken leg I mentioned before, got me to thinking that maybe I should expand, since everything depended on me. If I got incapacitated, the business would grind to a halt. Being a one-man shop taught me a lot though. I learned that if something was going to get done, I had to do it – from cleaning the toilet to selling and producing printing. So I put together a plan and sought an SBA loan, using as collateral our new house. I got the loan and hired an old friend as a salesman. The business continued to grow, and I moved the shop to a much bigger building. My younger brother Steve had bought an existing print shop in a neighboring town and we decided to merge as we had complimentary equipment which would let us do more in-house rather than farming it out. Business was good, life was good. I was married to the love of my life, had 3 healthy children, a nice house in a nice suburb, and a boat on Lake Erie. One night though, I was standing outside in late December, looking up at the sky, and was reminded of an old song sung by Peggy Lee: "Is That All There Is?" I wondered – it seemed as if I had everything a person could want, but there was something missing. I had been raised in Church, and we had been going to Church regularly since the children had some along – but was there to be something more?

Sally and I had been told about a couples retreat called "Marriage Encounter." We went to one and learned that it was all about communication, but more importantly, putting Christ at the center of your marriage. I had heard for years, watching Billy Graham crusades and other things that a person needed to have a personal relationship with Jesus as their Savior. I'm sure I had done that in some of the formal ways such as confirmation, but felt the need to do it again in my own way. On that weekend I said my own prayer inviting Jesus in to my life. There was no singing of angels or other dramatic signs - just the inner knowledge that I had done it. Some time later I went to a men's retreat called "Cursillo." It is spanish for "short course" which began in Spain to get men back involved in the Church. It was only in the Roman Catholic Church at the time, and had spread to the United States. Some friends and neighbors who were Roman Catholic had told us about it. Women were then allowed to go, but if married, their husbands had to go first. So, to please Sally, I went. I heard testimonies from men, and teaching from clergy. One Roman Catholic priest talked about God loving us in such a way as I had never heard before. I came out of that weekend knowing that something had changed in my life, but didn't know what that meant yet.

Seminary

I began praying regularly, asking God if He wanted me to do something else, to show me what it was, and I would do it. I talked to the priest at my church and to others, and I even wrote to Billy Graham for advice. He wrote back to me, although I don't remember what he said - I wish I had kept the letter. I had been very critical of the Episcopal Church as it had gotten very liberal. We heard a sermon about boycotting lettuce and Gallo wine. It seemed like we heard little Good News such as I had heard at Cursillo. One day as some of us were being critical, one lady ask me why I didn't do something about it? To me, that meant doing something from the inside, not just criticizing. I started to wonder if I should go to seminary. I talked to my priest about seminary, and asked "why me?" After all, as you have read, I had not been the best kid. He responded, "why not you?" I had no answer for that. The first brochure for a seminary he gave me was for the Episcopal Theological Seminary in Kentucky, in Lexington. I went down there for an interview, and was accepted. I sold my half of the business to my brother Steve, and we sold our house and moved our young family to a new town.

During the summer before we left, we visited my Grandmother Horr in Portsmouth. She had been bed ridden for years due to a heart ailment, but was always up on the latest news and the Cincinnati Reds season. She was always a delight to visit. When I told her about seminary, she said, "do you think I could have lain here all these years without a strong faith?" Grandmother was quite a lady, and you could see where my Mom got her personality.

Just before we moved, we bought a pop-up camper thinking that we probably wouldn't be able to afford fancy vacations for awhile. For several weeks after we moved to Lexington, the family took a camping trip all the way down to Florida, including time at Disney World. The camper was kind of cramped as we also had a teenage foster daughter at that time. I think the family enjoyed the trip though and we used that camper for several years even after we moved to Richmond.

Part of the process for being ordained was to get the permission of your bishop and eventually the Standing

Committee of the Diocese. I went to see the Bishop of Southern Ohio who told me that I would have to get my undergraduate degree before he would give me any financial assistance. I was now looking at 5 years before being ordained. One option I had was to attend seminary pursuing a licentiate in Theology, which was the same course but without the need for the an undergraduate degree. That was not an option in Southern Ohio, but I found that in the Diocese of Lexington where the seminary was, some people did that. We would have to move there and start school with no promise from the bishop or diocese of sponsorship. In an early interview with one of the examining chaplains in Lexington, I was told that he would recommend that I get my degree first. This was late summer, so I quickly began the enrollment process at UK. I found that all my credits would transfer from Ohio State, but not the grade average. It was like being given a fresh start. Also, I didn't have to pay out-of-state tuition! So I went to seminary during the day, and to UK classes at night and during the summer, and finished all 5 years of school in 3 years. During that time Sally started to work full time as it became clear that the monthly payments I got from the sale of the business was not enough. I also worked during my last summer and year at a print ship since my undergraduate work was finished. I ran presses and did other printing work, but when the owner found that I was handy with tools, had me doing various maintenance and remodeling work on the shop.

Needless to say this entire experience caused some stress in our lives. Not only did we have our three children, but the teenage foster daughter and eventually her brother, as well as several younger short term foster children from time to time. However, I was doing what I thought God wanted me to do, and was enjoying the process of pursuing ordination, with all the learning, testing and interviews with the excitement of eventually leading a church.

I mentioned earlier that a person who felt a call to ordination had to first get the approval of his local congregation, then his bishop. I had gotten the recommendation of the parish in Worthington, Ohio but not the bishop in Southern Ohio. Going to Lexington was an act of faith that I could get the approval of the Bishop of Lexington. However, I had to get approval of a congregation down there, as well as a Commission on Ministry, and the Standing Committee. Those had to be obtained before each part of the process - becoming a Candidate for Holy Orders, then ordination as a deacon, and eventually as a priest. All I knew was to keep plugging along and doing what was needed. One day early on the local bishop visited the seminary and suggested that we keep up with all assignments each day and there would never need to experience the panic that some students felt because they procrastinated. Fortunately, I had learned good work habits running my own business, so I kept up with all the reading and writing even though I was going to two educational institutions and pursuing two degrees. My grades in both were certainly much better that at OSU years before.

One place my work habits really helped was in the General Ordination Exams, or G.O.E.'s as they were called. Most seminarians dreaded them from their first year on. They come near the end of the last year, and are a week of essay questions that try to get a candidate to show what he has learned over the three years regarding all the book learning they received as applied to real life situations. There were lots of stories of all the planning different people took to prepare for the actual week, from having someone lined up to do the typing, to some wives actually leaving town for the week so as to not be a distraction. One of the best courses I ever took in high school was 10th grade typing. I have gotten more use of that skill over years than any other. Another great benefit to me was being used to not having peace and quiet all the time to do my studying. As the week went on, some guys were talking about all the drafts they would write to get their answers to suit them. I took a different approach. I did my research, then sat at the typewriter and typed out the essay once and turned it in. No more stress than a normal week as far as I was concerned.

It was typical according to those who had graduated and become ordained, for most to not pass at least some of their exams. If that happened, they were examined by the local Commission on Ministry to make sure they grasped what was needed to become a priest. You can imagine my excitement when I finally got the letter from the General Board of Examining Chaplains of the Episcopal Church which said that: "We, having been assigned as Examiners of Michael Murphy hereby testify that we have examined the said Candidate upon the subject matter prescribed in Title III. Canon 5. Sensible of our responsibility, we give our judgment as follows: On the basis of the General Ordination Examination the Candidate has demonstrated satisfactory proficiency in the subject matter appointed."

I had to read it several times, and had Sally read it to see if I read it right. The exam is very subjective, but that is the best outcome a person could receive. It is called "passing your GOE's. I was the only one in my class to get such a score and did not have to have any more testing, but sailed through the rest of the interviews for Deacon and 6 months later for Priest. Most had to wait a year before being ordained a priest unless they were in charge of a parish and passed all other exams and interviews. Since I had passed, I didn't have to wait and was ordained in May, 1978 after graduation from seminary, and later as priest in December of that year, at St. Paul's Church, Newport, KY.

One things our Diocese had Candidates do was to require them to memorize all of the Offices of Instruction in the 1928 Prayer Book before they were ordained. You had to meet with a senior member of the Commission on Ministry and recite them. Again, students were stressed about this, and waited until the spring of graduation, further adding to the stress level during that time. I decided to get a jump on this, so memorized the Offices and made an appointment to drive to Danville, KY to meet with the person who would examine me, in late summer before my senior year. I still remember driving down there with our second daughter Rebecca, who drilled me on the answers as we drove. It went without a hitch, so no stress for me on that issue the senior year.

It was a great treat to have so many family members come for the graduation and ordination. I had asked the old priest who married Sally and me to present me for ordination. Samuel U.J. Peard was the priest that served at the first Episcopal Church I had attended. Even though I was not a regular weekly worshiper, I was impressed at how he talked to people, rather than "preaching" each week. He had lots of wisdom from all his years of serving. He told me once when I talked to him about ordination, that there was a lot of pain in the ministry. I had no idea then what he was talking about.

Priest

The Bishop of Lexington had told those who were being ordained and had positions, to take a week or two off before starting the new job. Heck, I was ready to get to work, and besides that, needed the income. So I was ordained on Sunday evening, and showed up to work on Monday at St. Paul's. We had been interviewed a month or so earlier, and they decided to call us and we accepted. I can still remember Sally and I kneeling at the altar praying about this possible call right after our interview while the vestry was meeting to make a decision. They came in and said "yes" and so did we. It was a beautiful old stone church with stained glass windows and a pipe organ right in the inner city across from the courthouse. It had seen its better days, but had a nursery school attached with breathed some life into the place.

The parishioners were working on rehabbing the house, or the "rectory" that was a few blocks away, and we couldn't move yet for that reason as well as we wanted to wait until school was out for the kids. I took a cot up and spent some nights there so I wouldn't have to drive back and forth each day. It gave me a good chance to get to know the people there as they invited me to dinner. There were some loyal parishioners there who seemed to respond to my leadership and some new people seemed to find their way there. I'm sure my early sermons were terrible as I never imagined myself a preacher and always dreaded that part of the job.

In December the bishop came to St Paul's to ordain me as a priest and a local guy as a permanent deacon. The congregation went all out in providing a great meal and again much of my family and many friends came. It was a joyous occasion. Now I could celebrate Communion rather than picking up consecrated elements from a neighboring priest and doing a "Deacon's Mass," which was distributing bread and wine that another priest had consecrated and doing an abbreviated service. Celebrating Communion, or the Eucharist was always a highlight for me to be privileged to do.

While in Newport, I bought a motorcycle, much to Sally's chagrin. I would ride it around while taking communion to shut ins or just visiting. I wonder what some of the old timers thought about that. I always got some interesting comments when I rode over into Cincinnati on some errand.

The public schools did not impress us so we enrolled our kids in the local Roman Catholic school. The priest there as well as other Catholic clergy were very accepting and supporting of us. That decision didn't sit well with some of my parishioners who were teachers in the public school. The inner city of Newport was also not the best place to raise a family. The town used to be wide open for gambling and other "sins of the flesh" and there were still strip bars with signs advertising "miss nude Canada" or something like that. We did take a couple of nice vacations in our little Coleman camper though, once to Holden Beach, NC and one to Mammoth Cave, KY. One 4th of July Michael and I went down to the parish house and climbed up in the attic and then out onto the roof to watch the fireworks which were shot from the middle of the Ohio River. We could walk across a bridge which began right near the church across the Ohio River into Cincinnati. The Cincinnati Reds and the Bengals played in River Front Stadium right at the end of the bridge.

A program that was held while we were still living in Ohio at our local parish was called a Faith Alive. Lay people came for a weekend and during meetings, told about what their faith meant to them. It was a lay witness mission that got more people excited about their faith and their church. I always knew I wanted to have one of those when I got to serve a congregation. So plans were begun to have such a weekend at St. Paul's. There was lots of excitement as I worked with some men to spruce up the parish hall. We had gotten new carpet in the church, had the front doors painted red, and just made the place look more inviting. By then some more new people had come and we had a good turn out for the weekend. There seemed to be a new life in the congregation. However, some of the newer people had more trouble accepting the old members and were frankly very judgmental toward them. I was trying to minister to all people which ended up being a no-win situation. One afternoon two ladies came in to see me and spent an hour criticizing all aspects of the parish and what they perceived as my lack of leadership. I had been prone to get migraine headaches for some years, but they had been getting worse. That evening I got one so bad that it made me so sick that Sally got hold of a loyal member to come stay with the kids while she took me to the hospital. The personnel there called them "suicide headaches" and while I was in no danger of doing that, would have done almost anything to get rid of the pain. They gave me a shot of morphine which quickly got rid of the pain and provided great relief.

After that, I knew something had to give - that I could not try to make both those happy who wanted more renewal, and those who wanted things to stay more traditional. It came to a head at one vestry meeting where the vestry needed to reelect the Senior Warden. In that Diocese, the Senior Warden was traditionally called the "rector's warden and was nominated by him. One time the bishop told us seminarians that if the vestry would not elect who you as rector nominated, it might be a sign that you were losing your leadership and maybe a change was in order. They did not reelect the person I again nominated, a loyal member and good friend. I stopped the meeting then and told the vestry that. Soon after I let it be known that I was looking for a new position. Things calmed down but some of the people left and my heart was not in the place anymore.

After a several month search, and several interviews, we accepted a position with St. David's, in Richmond, VA. It was still a mission church, which meant it was newer and needed financial support from the Diocese. That also meant that the Bishop and Dept. of Mission still had more control over the affairs of the congregation, which is something I wanted to avoid. By the time I realized that, however, we had visited and liked the people we met and the location. At that time, I never could have foreseen that we'd spend 32 years in Virginia. That time produced lasting changes in our family.

It soon became evident that there was some discord between those who still lamented the change in the Prayer Book and those who weren't as concerned about that but wanted more renewal in the congregation including contemporary services. When I would offer a service that was in the new Prayer Book, such as the washing of feet on Maundy Thursday, some just couldn't stand that and either criticized me or left the church. I pushed for having the Eucharist each Sunday, but there were those who still loved Morning Prayer and fussed about that. I gave sermons at the 8 o'clock service which upset some folks. They just wanted to get in and out quickly. I stressed and taught stewardship which was important both for the spiritual health of the people, but also so the congregation could become self-supporting and eventually enlarge the building to give it room to grow. That always causes resistance which the bishop called "pocket book protection." We cut down some trees and painted the building white so it was more visible from the streets. Some complained about that and a few left.

As I mentioned before, Fr. Peard, who married us and presented me for ordination, always preached as if he was just talking to us. I never could see him refer to notes or a text. I always wanted to do that, but it seemed frightening to not have anything in front of me. Kind of what walking a tight rope without a net must feel like. I didn't want to get up in front of people and make a fool out of myself - the fear of public speaking that most people experience. However, just as with some other things I've done, I thought the best way do do this was just to do it. Since the Episcopal Church was a liturgical church, the time for sermons was only 15 minutes or less. That means I wouldn't have to produce a long, exhaustive talk, but would concentrate on making one main point in such a way as people might remember it. So I began by still doing much reading and thinking, and even attending a sermon support group for a time. Once I came up with the main point the lectionary lessons were trying to make, that would give me a theme. Then I would try to come up with some example to begin with which would help me illustrate the point and get people's interest. I would go over what I wanted to say in my head several times - even while I ran each morning. Then I would get comfortable enough with what I wanted to say so that I could just say it each week. I enjoyed preaching like that, and I hope people enjoyed that rather than have someone read a sermon to them.

We decided to have a Faith Alive at the congregation. There was lots of planning and work as a group of lay people came in and witnessed to their faith. We had good attendance all weekend. At the closing on Sunday evening we started with a couple of contemporary songs which was what was normally done. One long term stalwart member who had been a senior warden said he didn't want to sing anymore of those songs. I said that is what is usually done, at which time he and his wife stormed out, never to return. I thought the guy was supporting what we were trying to do there, so it was a surprise. There were others who also dug in to resist the direction the congregation was taking, including one woman who I came to label an antagonist, based on a book I read on the subject. Nothing would please her and she caused lots of dissension among the congregation as she was the wife of a founding member. It got so bad that I was ready to excommunicate her and even had a letter to the bishop typed and ready to mail regarding that.

I began to wonder if I had made a serious mistake with this entire ordination thing - did I mistake what God wanted me to do? I upset our nice comfortable life and drug my family hundreds of miles from the rest of our family just to endure this kind of grief? I called the bishop one day and quoted a line from a Johnny Paycheck song "you can take this job and shove it." A Vicar of a mission church technically works directly for the Bishop. He calmed me down and was very supportive to me. All this time though, some new people were coming in. About this time the woman mentioned previously as an antagonist left the church. She must have seen that the newer people were going to change the tide. It was what some clergy call a "blessed subtraction." Among new people coming in was a young family of which the man got elected to the vestry, and later a senior warden. He was very supportive and became a good friend as well. Another lady who at first was not so supportive became very helpful, and was also eventually elected as senior warden. She also eventually became active in the Diocese and worked with me as we began a new congregation in Virginia Beach and later in Chesterfield County.

This stronger lay leadership really helped the numbers of people and giving in the congregation grow and become self-supporting, There was a celebration at the Diocesan Council as the mission was accepted as a full parish, then back in the parish that evening. It was a major milestone in the life of the congregation and one that generated even more enthusiasm. After a year or so I suggested that the congregation should look into expanding the building. Too small a building would stifle the growth as has been evident in other congregations in the area. We hired a person experienced in fund raising and had a formal capital campaign. As usual, there were some who resisted, and to protect themselves and their wallets, they left. However, there was enough enthusiasm for the project, that enough was raised to double the worship space and add a large foyer. It wasn't all we had hoped for, but it helped the parish grow for the next several years as we could all worship together in the larger space.

During this time I had become a member of the Dept. Of Mission of the Diocese. This group oversaw the mission churches under the leadership of the Archdeacon and the Bishop. I was active in other Diocesan groups as well. In time I was appointed the chairman of the Department. I was beginning to think that in the future, when the current Archdeacon retired, I would like to have that job. Frankly, I was beginning to get somewhat bored with parish work, hence the Diocesan activity. I never particularly felt called to parish work, but that is how the system works - a priest has to put in his time there first. The parish was good to us though as my salary was increased and I felt much more support. They even gave me a trip to Israel in 1989 which was quite a great experience.

That made it harder for me to apply for the position of Archdeacon since things were going so well in the parish. I felt though that it would be better to make a change when things were going well, rather than the opposite. So I let it be known that I wanted that job, had an interview, and got a phone call one evening telling me that I was hired. I began January 1, 1990. Once a month I had to drive to Norfolk for staff meetings, and visited a different mission or small church each Sunday to preach and celebrate the Eucharist. I also met with churches for a variety of reasons, including trouble shooting or helping to find a new priest. Occasionally the bishop would assign me to a parish where there was an unhappy parting between priest and parish, to fill in for a time until he could appoint a regular interim priest. I also worked with some large congregations as a consultant in helping in their search process. One goal the Dept. Of Mission adopted under my leadership was to begin several new congregations in the Diocese. It was the Decade of Evangelism in the Episcopal Church, and we thought one way to reach people with the Gospel was to plant new churches. As mentioned previously, we began 2 new churches and purchased some land for future ones. I loved the job. I felt I was doing more to positively effect the larger church which is what I believed my original calling was. I liked not being tied down to a desk. I loved driving so enjoyed driving all over the southeastern third of Virginia visiting churches and clergy. I drove over 30,000 miles a year for the job. It could make for some late nights or long days as I drove home from night meetings or a Sunday service on the Eastern Shore.

I said before that the move to Virginia led to some big changes in our family. All three children graduated from High School, then College. Our daughters married two fine men who we are proud of. Our son went to Dental School then the Air Force where he met and married a great young woman. There are 10 grandchildren from those unions. We bought our second house in 1990 - the first after selling our house in Ohio in 1970 and going to seminary. We lived in that house 18 years.

I found that the bishop I worked for was an active alcoholic. Two staff members who were in Norfolk did an intervention on him to get him into treatment. After he returned to work, he was not the same. He had a mean streak that became more evident. He seemed to get paranoid, worrying about what people thought of him. One day he was coming up to the Richmond area to perform an ordination that evening. He called me and wanted to take me to dinner. I thought that would be nice to have a little one-on-one time with him. During dinner he told me that he was going to call for a Coadjutor Bishop. That was a bishop who had to be elected by the Diocese, and would succeed the Diocesan Bishop, who I worked for, when he retired. At first I thought that was good news, since as I alluded earlier, working for him was getting more difficult. Then he kept talking saying that for the Diocese to afford the large compensation package of the new bishop, two positions would have to be eliminated - mine and the part-time assistant bishop. He assured me that I would have all the time needed to find a new position. Needless to say, I was stunned. I had even come back from a sabbatical early to begin a new church in the county I lived in because there was so much interest in it.

I had asked the bishop to let me be the founding priest and do services there on Sundays rather than travel around the Diocese. I sat in the ordination later thinking that this person being ordained doesn't have a clue what was in store for them. The church can kick them aside no matter what sacrifices they made to get to that point.

Police Officer

I had been a volunteer police chaplain. I got to ride with officers anytime, to observe what they did, and was on call to make death notifications to next of kin. I really enjoyed getting to know cops. They seemed more authentic than many of the clergy I knew. I pretty much decided that I didn't want another church job - either in a parish or otherwise. Even if I had wanted another staff job, they were hard to come by for someone outside a diocese. People already in a diocese usually got those jobs because they were known. I went through some career counseling to try to determine what I wanted to do for the rest of my working life. I was 51 by this time, so had a good number of working years left. I kept thinking that I wanted to be a cop. However, the starting salary for police officers was 1/3 of what I was making as Archdeacon. I didn't think we could afford that or that Sally would like it. We had been getting close to the time she could stop working and this would mean she'd have to continue for some time longer. I wasn't too worried about the physical part of the academy or being a cop, since we had run for years and I was in decent shape. She went along with it, though. You'll have to ask her how she felt about this large change.

To get hired as a police officer was more difficult than getting ordained. However, the education process was not as long. I had already applied to be what was called a Special Police Officer, which was a full officer, part time, and not paid. They were given all the equipment, and rode with other full officers, or sometimes two of them together. They usually helped with special events, but could be out anytime. To do that I had to fill out an extensive application, had a full background check including a credit report, and an interview and polygraph. This took some time. When I changed to applying for a full time regular officer, all that had to be done again. Also there were a couple of more interviews for full-time. To begin the process for full time we had to pass a written test and if we passed that returned for the physical test later that day. The written test did more to test our powers of observation than anything else. They would show you a picture of a scene, then ask questions about that scene after the picture was taken away. There were several hundred people taking the test that morning. Then you would come back after lunch and see the posted results. If your name was on the list as having passed, then you took the physical test. There were many fewer at that point, but was still a sizable group. The physical test consisted of push ups, sit ups, and a mile and a half run. I had been working on all three for some time, so had no trouble passing. I was given notice by the bishop near the end of 1995, and applied to the county in early 1996. The Academy began in summer of 1996. I gave my notice to the Diocese, which was less than 2 weeks because of the Police Dept. taking so long to finish their process. I told the bishop that I discovered that I liked being around cops more than clergy. He didn't like that, but I didn't care.

So I, and over 20 other men showed up one hot July morning in our suits to attend the academy. We didn't know what to expect, but a number had been in the military, so probably had some idea what was coming. The academy was like boot camp but we went home at night so they couldn't mess with us more than the 8-9 hours we were there. Some of the guys who had been in the military said the academy was harder than boot camp. I found that hard to believe. It wasn't long before we were doing push ups on the hot pavement. Some guys got blisters on their hands it was so hot. I quickly learned not to look at the instructor when he was speaking and we were supposed to be at attention. He came over and got in my face for "eye balling" him. He called me in the office later and chewed me out some more. I told him I was used to looking at people when they were speaking. We wore our suits for a couple of days until we got our academy uniforms, which were just plain green work pants and shirts. Some of the guys showed us how to tuck in the shirt properly so it would not bag out, and to get our "cinch line" straight - the line from shirt buttons down to the fly on your pants. We would have to take our uniform to the cleaners and ask for military pressing, so all the seams looked sharp. We learned to spit shine our shoes and how to march.

Now I had been in Air Force ROTC at Ohio State and learned to stand at attention and the other various stances. I was even on the drill team for a time, so knew how to march, but was a little rusty. We spent lots of time marching each day for a few days. We would run each morning through the local neighborhood and eventually on trails in a nearby park. The problem was, believe it or not, I found I had to run early in the morning at home before I went to the academy because we could not leave anyone behind, and there were a few out of shape guys who were very slow. I didn't want to lose my conditioning. In addition we'd do calisthenics each day including mountain climbers and lifting weights. They would like to mess with us so they could yell at us more. One day after the morning formation and flag raising, we were all called outside from our class room. The county flag was upside down so we just got chewed out something awful. Problem was, it was put up right but they turned it around so they could accuse us of messing up.

Wasn't long before I figured out I would be able to take anything they would dish out. Fact is, they wanted us to succeed so weren't just going to wash someone out for no good reason. Once I got the gist of how things were supposed to be done, it was smooth sailing. They say that police work is hours of boredom interspersed with a few minutes of excitement. Our classes and exercises got us used to that. Most of the instructors were o.k. but not spell binding. And the practical exercises caused all of us to stand around and wait for our turn since there were so many of us. One of the most fun parts was shooting. Obviously they wanted you to be intimately acquainted with your weapon so we'd shoot often. It would all be timed and scored. For instance, they would say to draw and shoot 3 times, then draw and shoot 6 times, etc. We had to get a decent score in the allotted time. We'd have to practice shooting with our weak hand, standing, kneeling and lying down. The first few times most of us got blisters on our hands from the recoil of the gun. One guy complained that his sights must be off since he wasn't scoring well. The old instructor took his gun and shot several shots dead center, and handed the gun back to him. He said it wasn't the gun. Of course we'd have to clean the guns each day, but we weren't allowed to take them home yet. We also shot our 12 gauge shot guns regularly.

I made the mistake once of going in to see the instructor to tell him that I didn't agree with all the hazing that went on and didn't see the point in it. He told me that it was a way to break us down, then build us back up. The next day the head of the academy came out and chewed us all out for thinking we knew better than they did. I was not singled out, but I knew what caused his tirade.

One of the parts I dreaded was boxing. I was told early on that we would box each other. Now I had taken boxing one quarter at Ohio State for PE but it had been a long time since I got hit in the head. The day came and I had forgotten my mouth piece. I had to go to a nearby sporting goods store to buy another one. I was so nervous that my mouth piece made me gag, so I had to trim much of it off toward the back to prevent that. Then my turn finally came. I was up against a young guy who could bench press over 300 lbs. We sparred for a time, and I got in some good lefts, but never threw my right for some reason. I must have gotten hit, because that night when I went home my neck was stiff and store from the blows. Strange things is, the next day that young guy came in and quit the academy. I can't believe it was because of the punches I threw, but maybe he didn't like the idea of possibly being hit on the job.

We would also wrestle each other, using rubber knives as weapons. We'd take turns being the attacker and the other would defend himself. Then there would be two on one. I think I had a rib broken during one of those fights as a guy fell on my chest with his knee after they threw me down. It hurt badly so much that I couldn't do sit ups for a few weeks. I never reported it because that might mean I'd have to wait until the next academy. There would be all kinds of other physical activities to get us into shape and test us. One was defensive tactics. That was also no fun since we could get hurt as we got thrown to the mat. We learned all kind of pressure points and ways to bend a person's arm or wrist to cause pain and thus compliance if they were struggling. We were not supposed to be offensive, but able to defend ourselves if we got attacked. I hardly ever had to be physical with a suspect so didn't need that training much. Maybe since I was older they thought I was a wily old cop who would thrash them. I always tried to treat people firmly with respect unless they escalated the situation, so maybe that helped.

One of the fun parts but most stressful of the academy was driving. You had to be able to drive the car around a cone course, which included backing into tight spaces. It was timed. I wondered if I would pass because they would not let you use your mirrors to back up, which I was used to. I knocked down plenty of cones. I guess I finally made it. A more fun part was pursuit driving. We went out to Fort Picket and took turns being the chase car or the one being chased. Again there were cones, but we learned how to take the curves the fastest and that it was hard to roll a car over unless you hit something. I remember the satisfaction of staying right on the tail of a high ranking officer. I don't think he liked it that he couldn't lose me. Of course driving was one skill we used all the time on the job, although I was only in two pursuits.

As graduation drew near, the instructor called me into his office and told me that at first he didn't think I could hack it in the academy but I proved him wrong. I felt pretty good about that. The graduation ceremony was nice and some family and friends attended. Then we were to begin our 8 weeks of field training. That consisted of 2 weeks on day shift, 2 on midnight, and 4 on evening. We would have a different Field Training Officer for each session. The first two days of the first 2 weeks the FTO would drive, then we drove all the time. The training was supposed to be instructional, but we were graded on it as well.

I felt like a klutz for a time - just finding my way around different parts of the county using a map was hard even though we had lived there for some years by then. One day I had stopped a car, and my shoe lace caught on a bracket on the car door causing me to trip as I exited. My FTO told me I wasn't having a good day. You had to be able to think fast in any situation and make decisions quickly on what to do - sometimes life and death decisions. You had to project firmness and certainty or people would not follow your instructions. Of course you had to know the law, especially the laws of arrest so you didn't arrest someone without a warrant that didn't fit that criteria and then get charged with false arrest. The job of a police officer is extremely complicated with all you have to know, as well as all the tactics to use to keep yourself safe.

The second section of field training was in the south part of the county for evening shift. The FTO I had wanted me to drive with my hands placed at 10 and 2 - both hands on the wheel. Now I had been driving for a long time and hadn't used both hands often, especially at 10 & 2. He was also very critical of other things, and had his own way of doing things. It was even more difficult to find my way around that part of the county as I had lived in the north end for years.

The third section was also evening shift but again in the north part of the county. This was another FTO. He had been undercover for a time, and was much more aggressive in dealing with people. One night he wanted to teach me how to cut over the median on a 4 lane road and reverse direction without waiting for a paved cut through, without getting stuck or hitting an oncoming car. He showed me a couple of times, then let me drive. The time came when he told me to start, and I think I wasn't going fast enough as he started yelling to speed up so we wouldn't get stuck, then he yelled because an approaching car was getting too close and he was afraid we'd hit it. We didn't get stuck or hit, but I don't remember ever trying that again when I was on my own.

One night we got a call about men with guns in a neighborhood. We arrived and were talking to the complainant when he yelled "there they are." They were three young black males who had guns stuck down the front of their pants. I didn't have my gun out yet, but I noticed that my FTO and another officer did. He yelled at me to get my stuff out! We yelled at them to stop which they did, and got them down on the ground at gun point. They were yelling "Rodney King, Rodney King" recalling the guy in LA who some said was mistreated by the police after he ignored their orders. The guys all had BB guns, but they looked so real if they had pulled them out and swung them our way, we would have shot them.

Then came the midnight shift in the north end. I was going to end up on midnight shift, which is what I wanted. I liked the idea of being able to patrol around with less traffic, as well as it not being so hot in the summer. Wearing the body armor was something I promised Sally I'd do, but it was not comfortable. My FTO was a small guy but was on the Swat team and also a helicopter pilot in the National Guard. DUI's were a big thing on midnight shift, so he had me patrol around the main highways for the first part of the shift and watch for drivers who were swerving or doing other things that would lead you to think they might be intoxicated. My FTO really did a good job of guiding me through all the steps in dealing with DUI's. I won't go into all the process here, but it was complicated to first determine that a person might have been drinking, then a do a field sobriety test, then a portable breath test, then to take them to the magistrate's office to do an official breath test, then in front of the magistrate who would order them taken to jail if he agreed with you. And of course you had to take notes soon after so you could testify in court and get a conviction. You first had to testify as to your reason for stopping the car, then go from there. The prosecutor should guide you through the steps, but some were better than others. Of course you had to do all the steps in the actual stop, arrest and transport in a safe manner because drunks were unpredictable.

As mentioned earlier, I seldom had to get physical with people, but had to be ready to if needed. One guy I saw was pushing his car since it has stalled. I stopped to see if he needed help, and could smell that he was drunk. He had been driving, and was still in control of his car, so I gave him the tests, and the portable breath test. I began to place him under arrest but he struggled. Now by this point in most DUI stops, another officer is backing you up. The suspect had no shirt on, so we bent him over the hot hood of my police car, which caused him to immediately stop resisting. Strange thing is that I arrested the same guy some time later, and when I went to court for that charge, was told he had committed suicide.

One time I had a drunk woman try to get the car door open and jump out as we were driving down a highway at a high rate of speed to jail. I grabbed her arm and held on so tight that she must have had bruises. I was glad she never tried to accuse me of police brutality. You might wonder how someone could get a door open. The county didn't have cages in the back with doors that wouldn't open from the inside. We had to handcuff the prisoner and put them in the front seat beside us. One guy that we had to wrestle to get under control was squirming around as we drove to jail. I asked him what he was trying to do, and he said he was trying to get his pants down so he could sh-t in my car. He did lots of cussing me out, so when in court later the judge asked, as he always did, if the person was cooperative, I told him exactly how the guy behaved and what he said. There was some snickering back in the court room. The judge gave the guy the maximum sentence he could. There are lots of drunk stories in my 4 years on midnight shift. I got so I wished that rather than have to go through all the steps leading up to the arrest and then recounting them in my testimony in front of the judge, that I could just say, "your honor, I deal with drunks all the time and I know when they are drunk. This guy was drunk." But, lawyers write many of the laws, and the complicated system that was set up for DUI convictions kept some of them in business.

In the academy we had several days instruction on DUI's. A State Trooper taught the classes. One of the things we had to do was to drink a measured amount of alcohol, then be tested by a class mate who wasn't drinking. Needless to say, half of us drank one day and the other half tested, then we reversed the next day. We were assigned a buddy to take us home, then we'd take him home the next day. I was amazed at the amount of alcohol I could drink and not be legally drunk. So I was amazed one night when I pulled over a person I suspected of being drunk, and as he got out of his truck, he said, "you got me, I just finished a 12 pack." That sure would have meant he was legally intoxicated, and he was.

I hardly ever had to pull my gun on anyone. One time on day shift, I got a call to arrest a person who had a felony warrant. Felony stops were high risk stops that entailed getting the person out of the car at gun point and down on the ground where they could be cuffed while another officer kept a gun on them. Then you could search them. For this call, the person was in a parking lot and out of his car as I drove up. There were several other people around, and I had no back up yet. I pulled my gun on the suspect and then ordered others in the area to stand still. Everyone complied and I got the suspect cuffed and placed in my car. On the way to the jail he told me that he didn't try anything on me because I "had the eye." I asked him what that meant, and he told me that the look on my face indicated to him that I meant business. I've thought since that trait must have been inherited from my Dad, as I remember he could give quite a stern look at times.

Another time I happened to be at the North precinct when an armed robbery call came out - just down the road from where I was. I got in my car as another officer in the area headed that way, and just down the road from where the robbery happened, we saw the suspect vehicle. We did a felony stop and by the time we got out of our cars, lots of other cops were there. There were three guys in the car, so we got them out one at a time. When I got the third one out and face down and cuffed I rolled him over to begin the search and found a gun in the front of his pants. That was a good lesson in following procedure and relying on our training to keep something serious from happening. I don't know what ever happened to those three as we turned them over to detectives, but they were found with the stolen stuff on them so it should have been a slam dunk case.

I enjoyed midnight shift as I could patrol around late at night. If I got tired, I would get out of the car and walk around a school or some other public place, kind of the way you see on TV when cops walk a beat. One night I was checking out a neighborhood pool where kids would sneak in. Suddenly I heard some yelling and splashing then running as a couple saw me coming so got out of the pool quickly and ran off,. They ran down to a lake and I could hear them splashing as they ran down the shore to get away. I wasn't going into the water for a minor trespassing charge, so went back to the pool where I found their clothes. I took them and hid them in the lost and found. I always wondered how those kids explained showing up at home naked in the middle of the night.

One time Sally and I were driving home from visiting our daughter in Tennessee when Sally's cell phone rang with our son on the other end asking where I was. She told him I was right beside her in the car. He called because he heard on the news that a Chesterfield County officer had been shot and killed and wanted to make sure that it wasn't me. It was kind of a surreal experience for me, as I had dealt with the suspect who did the shooting. He was kind of a strange guy who would cause trouble in the neighborhood. I had to deal with him when I was on midnight shift, but never had cause to arrest him. This time a gun was involved, and the young rookie officer walked up to his house and knocked on the door. The guy opened the door and shot the officer just as he turned away. The bullet went under his arm where there was no protection from the vest. Again I wondered about the circumstances - the same guy in the same beat. If I had been working, even though I was then on day shift, the call came in late on the midnight shift so I could have been responding due to the shift overlap.

I was in only one pursuit that was initiated by me, but it was not the high speed kind you see on TV. I was in the country late at night and saw a big BMW sedan run a stop sign. I turned around and turned on my blue lights to stop him, but he didn't stop. He wasn't going fast, but just would not stop. So I turned on my siren but still he kept going. There are certain procedures you have to do when initiating and maintaining a pursuit. First you have to declare that you are in pursuit. That gives you total access to the radio so there are no more calls being given out or other routine talking. Then you have to advise the speed that you are going, and weather and traffic conditions as well as your location as that changes. The driver just wouldn't stop, and I felt kind of silly advising dispatch that he was only going 35-45 MPH. He just kept going up and down country roads. It wasn't long until there were several other officers in line, including the shift lieutenant. After some time, the guy turned off the road into a driveway that led up into a field, then jumped out of his car and ran into the woods. It wasn't long before we saw him hiding behind a tree, and got him cuffed without further incident. The guy was a middle aged man who happened to be driving on a suspended license. It would have been more exciting if he was a decent driver.

The only other pursuit I was in I was about third in line. It was a much higher speed pursuit more like you might see on TV, with sparks flying as the cars bottomed out going over bumps in the road and squealing tires going around corners. Finally a State Trooper got involved and was able to physically force the car off the road, where he was caught. We were not allowed to use our cars to strike another car, so it was nice to have the Trooper end the pursuit. It was just some kid being stupid in public and running from the cops rather than facing a traffic ticket.

As time goes on, most cops do other things than patrol. It

is the rare cop that spends his whole career patrolling. That is nothing negative about them because it is important to have seasoned people out on the road. The street cop is normally the first one to respond to whatever happens, whether a traffic accident or crime in progress. They also discover many crimes that never would have been found, and prevent many crimes from happening just by being out there. Some cops don't like to do traffic stops, but much crime is prevented or discovered by doing just that. I enjoyed running radar when I could because it was kind of like hunting or fishing. You would sit and wait for the "game" then you had to pull out safely then drive full-out until you caught up with the speeder, then be able to stop as they pulled over without hitting them. I found drugs, concealed weapons, and people with active warrants among other things. One night I stopped a car and as I walked up to it noticed that the license plate holder has some type of Biblical quote on it and said "Pastor's Wife." I thought it might be a pleasant stop. The lady began cussing me out so strongly that I was shocked. She refused to sign the summons but when I explained to her that if she didn't, I would have to arrest her and take her to the magistrate, she finally relented. The next day I got a call from her husband who tried to get me to fix the ticket. I told him that if she went to court, I would tell the judge how she acted. She just paid the ticket. Goes to show how you just never know about people.

I applied to do marine patrol on Lake Chesdin. The department would put trained officers in a boat to enforce laws on the lake, including drunk boat operating. This usually happened only on weekends or holidays, so you had to pull your normal shifts on other times. I had owned a boat on Lake Erie, and was used to all kinds of weather and navigation conditions, as well as rules of the road. I thought it would be a slam dunk to get that position which would give some variety to just patrolling. I didn't get the job. I applied for a detective position, thinking that might be a change of pace. I didn't get the job. One summer, after I volunteered to assist doing background checks on new hires, I got called to help out those detectives. I found the job to be tedious as you had to track down every lead in finding out as much as possible on candidates. It was not the exciting job you see on TV, and with our department you didn't even get a pay raise. I forget how many people I had to investigate in the beginning, but only one got hired.

I took the sergeants test twice, including interviews. I scored high enough each time to get on the short list, but both times they were not hiring more than one or two. There was an opening for a crime prevention officer. The job entailed public speaking, and since I had about 18 years experience by then in public speaking, I thought I could get that job, which would be a nice change of pace. They hired another guy first, then hired me to do the citizens academy. I thought that might be enjoyable, but soon found that any secretary could do that job. That is why when a person from a neighboring town called me one summer evening in 2004 to see if I would be interested in being their priest, I said I would talk to them. I never expected to be back in church work.

Priest 2

I had an interview with what was called the Cure Vestry - a Cure was a group of churches banded together so they could afford a priest. Some of the people of the group I had known and liked from my years in the diocese, especially as the Archdeacon. I was also familiar with the area from the previous job, and my bike riding in the country. We could remain in our house, as the counties the two churches were in were adjacent to ours. It was an easy interview for me since I didn't need a job, and didn't seek this one out. I could just be myself and say what I thought. I was able to officially retire from the Police Dept. with a small pension. I was still ambivalent about making the change back to church work, but this position intrigued me. There wouldn't be the pressure to worry about making the church grow, but only involved two Sunday services and pastoral care. We decided it would be approximately 4/5 time, however you figured that out. I talked with my son-in-law about it while on vacation that October, and I decided to decline the job. When we got back home, I called the person who originally called me, to let him know. He almost begged me to reconsider, so I met with him and another lady who was the senior lay person in the other church for one last meeting. I don't know what happened, but when I went home I told Sally that I took the job. She was very surprised. That ended 8 1/2 years as a cop. I always told people the jobs were similar - both heard confessions.

I began work at the first of Advent in 2004 only doing Sunday services, and the Christmas Eve services. Then on January 1, 2005 I began the 4/5 time job, doing what visiting needed doing, including new people, hospital visits, weddings, funerals, etc. As well as preaching twice each week and also extra Lenten services. It was over-all a good experience as the people seemed to enjoy my preaching which was mixed with cop stories. Both churches showed some growth and I felt I was treated very well. One congregation even totally made over the church office complete with new furniture which made it very comfortable.

Two big health events took place for us during my tenure at the Cure. Sally had been told for years that she had an irregular heart beat. She had been seen by a cardiologist who finally told her that she would need surgery to repair or replace a heart valve. That was done in 2007 as a repair. I won't tell her story here. For me, it was probably the worst thing I've ever experienced to see her right after surgery hooked up to all the machines. She was a trooper though, and as soon as possible, we walked around the hospital corridor, then around our block at home, then eventually 3 plus miles. We still walk and hike.

In 2008 during a regular check up my doctor said I should see a Urologist due to the PSA test jumping a point over the last year. I had a biopsy and was diagnosed with Prostate Cancer of the kind that needed some intervention or it would end up in my bones. "Watchful waiting" was not an option for me. I chose surgery with the DaVinci robot. My urologist told me this would be a bump in the road. After the experience, I would call it a huge pot hole. I only missed one Sunday doing service and was running again after two weeks. Sally was extremely understanding and helpful and at this writing after 9 years, I have been cancer free. I won't go into all the details of the recovery here, but only to let all my male blood relatives know that they should get checked beginning at age 40, not the usual 50, according to my urologist. There are some genetic factors involved in this disease.

Since the congregations were made up of older people, I had more funerals than I had at my other congregations. In fact, in 2010, which ended up being the last year I served, both Senior Wardens, one from each congregation, got cancer and died. The fact of ministering to two good friends during their illness, then doing their funeral, was not enjoyable. I decided that I didn't want to do that anymore, so after talking to Sally, decided to announce my retirement. I did Christmas Eve services in 2010 but there was a Sunday left in the year which would have been my last services. It snowed, so services were canceled, so I never really said good bye to the people.

Retirement

I mentioned earlier that Sally and I would fantasize while ice skating about hitching a ride on a train and seeing the country, and that as we decided to buy an RV after our retirement, that was kind of fulfilling that dream. We liked the idea of sleeping in our own beds, and taking our dog Joy with us. We have gone through several RV's since retirement trying to find the one that best suits us, but in all that time we have traveled many parts of the country seeing sights that many people don't see from the freeway, or air. There have been many "normal" sights, plus some big trips, such as to Yellowstone, Glacier, and Maine. In most places we try to find someplace to hike or walk with our dog that gives us a more up close look at parts of the country. We originally wanted to stay on the back roads rather than the freeways, but that is not always practical with the unit we have now. Some of the RV parks are very nice, and some are not. I research where we want to go and make reservations, as RVing has become much more popular since fuel prices have dropped. When we first started, we would just head out and go until we wanted to stop, then try to find a park. Some of them were less than adequate. Now, even with my research, some are less than adequate. We have met some very interesting and nice people, and seen some great sights. We're fortunate that in addition to loving each other, we like each other. It could be rough spending so much time together if we didn't get along well. When we will stop doing this remains to be seen. So far we enjoy it and we're able to do it. However, when we stop, we'll find something else to do.

Two huge losses occurred in 2012: my Mom died in January, and my younger brother Scott died in November. Mom had suffered Alzheimer's for a number of years, and Scott developed some type of cancer that began in the bile tract and spread. Mom was a gracious, beautiful woman so it was difficult to see her decline like she did. Scott was an Air Force career officer who I felt close to since we were closer in age. We got to spend time in later years meeting up with our wives in some neat location such as the Outer Banks or the Eastern Shore, or at each others homes. He fought the cancer for some time but it won out in the end. Part of his ashes are buried at Arlington.

As my Mom got more disabled she had to be moved to an Alzheimer's unit at the place where she and Dad lived. When that happened, Dad moved his living quarters so he could visit her easier without a long walk or drive. As Mom got so she couldn't feed herself, Dad would go for each meal and feed her. He finally got the facility to give him his meals with Mom. He did that until she died - seeing her at least 3 times a day. What an example of love and devotion he gave to us all.

My Dad died in May, 2017. Dad had quite a decline that began in early 2017. Up to then, even with a pace maker and catheter, he was mentally active and would get around his housing unit as needed. He had moved back to his hometown after my Mom died and my brother Steve found a very nice place for him to live. Then this decline began. We were planning on visiting him in April, but in early March we decided we should go due to his decline. On that visit, he never got out of bed, but did talk some and even told a joke. We only stayed about an hour before he seemed very tired so we headed out, and as we left, I knew it would probably be the last time I would see him. For some time, Dad didn't like to say good-bye, but "I'll see you" or "until next time." Most of us got into that practice too. When I told him "until next time" he had a little smile, and said the same thing. I was never able after that to speak to him on the phone. He died on May 21. Dad gave all the males in our family a great example of what a dad, husband and a man should be.

I want to say how wonderful my life with Sally has been. I could never have imagined that our love would grow to this extent. I also want to say how grateful I am for our three children, Sarah, Rebecca and Michael, Jr. I am amazed at the wonderful people they have turned out to be, and with their great spouses, have raised and are raising ten fine grandchildren. I certainly give thanks to God for them all.

I'll end with a line that ends a song by the Boothe Brothers called "In Christ Alone." It says: "In every victory, let it be said of me, my source of strength, my source of hope is Christ alone."

Made in the USA
Columbia, SC
26 December 2024

50622322R00035